Consider each of the affirmations on the following pages. Take a few minutes each day to jot down your thoughts, feel free to skip to ones that resonant depending on your mood.

For more inspiration

www.radiancetherapy.co.uk
Instagram:@radiance_therapy
Instagram: @radiance_the_lifestyle
Twitter: @sarahatradiance
Facebook: Radiance - Aromatherapy &
Reflexology
Facebook: Radiance-a lifestyle plan

I am strong

How does this make you feel?

_____

_____

_____

_____

_____

_____

_____

_____

_____

_____

_____

_____

_____

_____

_____

_____

_____

_____

My mind & body are still

Is this true?

I matter

How do you know this?

I take care of myself

How do you make sure of this?

I give myself permission to slow down

How do you make sure of this?

I choose to be happy
& love myself

Amazing, write 5 things to show this

I give myself permission to relax

What are you going to do to honour this?

_____

_____

_____

_____

_____

_____

_____

_____

_____

_____

_____

_____

_____

_____

_____

_____

_____

_____

I am making me
a priority

How will you ensure this happens?

I am relaxing, resting & calm

How and why?

Every day brings me new opportunities

Exciting, what are they?

I have goals

Set them here

_____

_____

_____

_____

_____

_____

_____

_____

_____

_____

_____

_____

_____

_____

_____

_____

_____

_____

_____

_____

I achieve what I set
my mind to

I achieve when I have a plan

Is it detailed?

I am not alone

Who is do you trust?

I am happy in my own company

What I like to do when on my own

When I meet friends I feel.

Explore this?

I am creative

How do you show this?

I am caring

You are, but who cares for you?

I am kind

How do you honour this?

I give myself permission to..

Do what?

Every day starts with a smile

Every day ends with a smile

I am abundant with gratitude

What 5 things are you grateful for right now?

I am flourishing

You are amazing

There is no such thing
as a mistake,
it is a lesson to grow from

Think about a situation you have learnt from

My status does not define me

You might be a sister, a daughter,
a mother, a wife, but who are YOU

I am more than I appear on the outside

This is your space, what is the one thing very few know about you?

Emotional release makes me stronger

What do you need to let go?

I am courageous

When did you last demonstrate this?

I am brave

When did you last feel butterflies
but showed some bravery?

I am unique

Yes!

My health challenges
make me a warrior

How?

I never give up

Progress not perfection

Curve balls will hit you,
how do you overcome them?

I day dream

Create your dream life,
what does it look like,
who is with you,
where are you?

I visualise my future, it is exciting

Could some (or all) of your dream life become reality?

I am capable of anything
I choose to do

I find joy in

List 10 things you love to do?

I know why I am here

Can you put it into words?

My challenges are..

Crying is not a weakness.

When did you last cry, why and how did you feel afterwards?

My home is my safe space.

What does 'home' mean for you?

My body is amazing.

Write down how fabulous it is?

I make a difference

Who to and how?

The last few pages are blank for your own thoughts.

Do you have affirmations of your own?
Dreams you would like to note?

Printed in Great Britain
by Amazon